YOUR WORLD MY MIND

BY

SAM THE WORD

Published 2023: Golden Child Promotions Publishing Ltd
Portland House, Belmont Business Park, Durham,
DH1 1TW

Onlygold@goldenchildpromotionspublishing.com

Copyright © 2024 by Sam The Word.

All rights reserved. No part of this publication may be reproduced, stored in a retrieval system or transmitted in any form or by any means, electronic, mechanical, photocopying, recording, and/or otherwise without prior written permission of the publishers.

This book may not be lent, resold, hired out or otherwise disposed of by way of trade in any form, binding or cover other than that in which it is published, without the prior consent of the publishers.

CONTENTS

ACKNOWLEDGMENTS 6

A NOTE FROM THE AUTHOR 9

INTRODUCTION 11

CHAPTER 1: THE VAGRANT 13

CHAPTER 2: DO I LOVE YOU? 15

CHAPTER 3: MISPLACED TRUST 18

CHAPTER 4: THE ASYLUM SEEKER 20

CHAPTER 5: THE SQUARE'S TALE 23

CHAPTER 6: BEAUTIFUL WOMAN 25

CHAPTER 7: TEARS OF A FOOL 27

CHAPTER 8: MY SON 30

CHAPTER 9: MISUNDERSTOOD 33

CHAPTER 10: THE DARK SIDE OF LOVE 36

CHAPTER 11: MR BELLYFULL 38

CHAPTER 12: GRANDAD WINT 41

CHAPTER 13: MUMMY WINT 43

CHAPTER 14: NERISSA WINT 45

CHAPTER 15: KIDS 47

CHAPTER 16: GRIME 48

CHAPTER 17: A SAD AFFAIR 52

CHAPTER 18: MY SHAME ... 56

CHAPTER 19: ASKING FOR FORGIVENESS ... 56

CHAPTER 20: TRUTH LOCKED DOWN ... 58

CHAPTER 21: FALSEHOOD ... 59

CHAPTER 22: THE MELANATED JOURNEY - THE DARK WOMB ... 60

CHAPTER 23: TIDA ... 64

CHAPTER 24: BOURNEMOUTH ... 65

CHAPTER 25: DON'T CUT ME ... 66

CHAPTER 26: DEVIL SHIP ... 68

CHAPTER 27: MISSING ... 69

CHAPTER 28: MADAGASCAN GIRL ... 70

CHAPTER 29: TOP HAT AND TAILS ... 71

CHAPTER 30: DOUBLE HARVEST ... 73

CHAPTER 31: ASSIMILATION ... 75

CHAPTER 32: LOST FOR WORDS ... 77

CHAPTER 33: HEARTS & MINDS ... 79

CHAPTER 34: HOW ARE YOU GONNA GET OUT OF THIS ONE? ... 83

CHAPTER 35: ORPHANS FOR DIAMONDS ... 86

CHAPTER 36: TATTOOS OF A BEDOUIN ... 87

CHAPTER 37: FEATHERED FRIENDS ... 88

CHAPTER 38: A WORD TO YOUNG GIRLS ... 89

CHAPTER 39: AFRICA'S HOLOCAUST _____ 92

CHAPTER 40: CALAA BAAJ _____ 94

CHAPTER 41: MARTIAN INQUISITION _____ 95

CHAPTER 42: SHANTY TOWN _____ 96

CHAPTER 43: FICKLE _____ 98

CHAPTER 44: LET ME REIGN _____ 100

CHAPTER 45: ONCE YOU HAD ME _____ 101

CONCLUSION _____ 105

ABOUT THE AUTHOR _____ 106

ACKNOWLEDGMENTS

My acknowledgments are for Golden Child Promotions Publishing, who gave me a platform and great motivation to steam ahead with getting published; My mom, who invested in me and took pride in my ancestry and hue. My teacher, Miss Parkin, who cried when my poem, The Tramp, my only work presented that year, was published in the area magazine.

My dad because he had some purpose in getting me here.

Sharon Frederick, she read so much good and incomplete work, but she gave me the attention I needed at the time. My dear, OG ride-or-die beautiful wife, Surraya Hemmings, who has put up with my crap for years and is also still looking for some of my misplaced writings, I blamed her for losing. She's a legend.

Warsan Shire, the poetess who has never heard of me, but her fabulous work inspired me to write Words with Wings and become a better writer; another inspiration came from Benjamin Folks, the English gent whose style inspired me to write the poem Arab Spring, when a teacher at HMP Dovegate challenged I could not write such a poem, let alone in a 1-hour lesson.

I'd like to thank Linton Kwesi Johnson, Ms. Lou, and Marcus Garvey, who gave me the passion and spirit of our Jamaican ancestry; Amatullah Tijuana Clark and Mumzy, who I almost drove to madness trying to explain to me how to file and open a new Chrome account to send much-anticipated writings by email, and my children whom I neglected when engrossed in getting this to the public.

I would also like to thank Arabella at Kestrel Org and Holly from the Royal Court Theatre in London, who helped me write scripts and act on stage, namely Blood and Water, as well as Co-star in the budgeted film The 360° Man.

I'd acknowledge Chicken Shed, who gave me one of my first audiences putting on a talent show at Warren Hill prison. The Koestler Awards, who awarded me many acknowledgments, and Gems Educational Trust, who gave me a commendation for the recitation of my penned poem once you had me.

Albany Music Group, who helped me get awarded for The Dark Womb. Apples and Snakes, who loved my work sessions and provided certification. My daughter, Kamilla Ahmed Samuel, for loving my work and collaborating with the poem and song The Open Prison.

Rasheed Khan, who loved my work and was highly spirited that I should publish. He has been a great support throughout my life.

Asmara Brown, who is amazing.

Baa, the main man, and owner of Golden Child Publishing. Cyrlene Braithwaite who introduced me to Golden Child Promotions Publishing, a dear friend, and member of the management team at Golden Child Publishing and owner of Britain's Got Reggae.

And last but not least, all the guys at Springhill Prison that put up with my demands and moaning, who helped me put music to lyrical expression or helped me find my work in either one computer or another. Mostly, Ricardo (aka CH) from the Johnnies - a magnificent poet and rap talent.

My friends like Marcus Ellis, Double, Chung Gregory, and Two Three, (The Burger Bar Man-dem) and Gary Notorious Nelson) who encouraged me to tell stories on lifer days. My brother Abdul Rasheed and Abu Baker who loved my nighttime stories when we should have been sleeping. Those prisoners of Whitemoor from Al Qaeda and the IRA whose names I will not mention, who cried when I recited Africa's Holocaust and Red Roses White Lilies.

To all those I didn't name here, the love is too numerous to mention but thank you also; as for the others, kiss my black one.

The poems the Grime and Hearts and minds were written in 2003-5, the pictures enclosed are from my first time picking up a paint brush in HMP Dove gate around 2011.

A NOTE FROM THE AUTHOR

I sincerely hope you enjoy this collection of poems. The Tramp was my first poem, although slightly edited on one line because I couldn't quite remember the original. I was nine and never did a stroke of work for months, but somehow it got me in the area magazine, which brought my teacher Miss Parkins to tears.

I wrote The Tramp because of a poor soul I saw who used to knock on doors for sausage and eggs. Sometimes I'd see him in the park in very cold weather, and one particular time, he looked so pale as if he had died from hypothermia. I suppose I was a little more socially aware for my age than what was the norm for someone my age.

I didn't write again for about thirteen years when I heard a poem by WH Auden, Stop All the Clocks. That was it for me. I tried to capture the style and write The Last Rites. It was my first attempt at such a style. I know it could hardly do Auden's Stop All the Clocks justice, but it stated my artistic license for writing and my appreciation for greatness. I added The Last Rites more as a record of my development than thinking I was somehow on par with delusional excellence.

I moved on to Africa's Holocaust after igniting the fire in me after watching Roots and reading books on slavery. I remember the Deputy head, Mr. Anderson, an ex-CID officer attempting to cane me for smashing up Walter Hill for attacking me for exposing his lies that he was with Sonya Swebe, the Choreographer for Andrew Lloyd Webber productions.

Anyway, I grabbed the descending cane, broke it in half, threw it in his face, and shouted, "White boy, my name is Kunta Kenti, not bloodclart Toby. Never raise your hands to me," and I left. I wrote an extensive poem about black Jesus which got corrupted in my personal organizer that I have since lost. Africa's Holocaust is based on all my experiences of racism from teachers, such as favoritism towards white children and having to fight bullies in Oakham in an all-white primary school. I read books by Ivan Sertima, Chancellor Williams, and Augustus Rogers, and papers by Drusella Andrews, Elijah Muhammad's Message to the Blackman, Malcolm X, and Marcus Garvey, to name a few. Africa's Holocaust is to make known to the world the biggest Holocaust of any race is indeed the black Holocaust which redneck crackers try to sweep under the bloody carpet of history. I will not allow it. I cannot allow it. I have no will to be silenced. I have nothing, had nothing, and so if me not achieving anything to please a racist audience is me compromising my race regarding the blemish stain and stench of racist, murderous tyrants and their treatment of black and darker races, I will not be silenced or ever have anything but my integrity. So, Africa's Holocaust is that poem that satisfies my passion for truth, and at the same time, it is an homage to all the fallen and those still suffering because we are melanated.

INTRODUCTION

I am a man from the East Midlands or Middle Earth, as Leicester is the golden /geographical meme of England. I started writing 27 years ago but gave up when my digital organizer malfunctioned, wiping out my favorite poem about black Jesus.

After becoming remanded at Doncaster Category A prison in the year 2000, only to lose two well-loved poems when being forcibly moved to the Beirut Wing, a couple of years after I was given a life sentence, I started writing again, mostly without realizing poetry was an art and novels had grammar and punctuation rules. Being anti-establishment, I didn't care much for conformity. Fearing I would lose a certain truth because of this affront to expression, I plodded on, and although I have gained a TEFL English teaching certificate, I still predominantly write as I think and feel. However, I can now appreciate why English is tutorially structured.

I hope you will like my abstract style of writing and the realism and, at times, the humor.

Indeed, I hope the socio-political and historical value will be a welcome breath of fresh air as too often fuddy-duddy pretentious poems and prose also got up my nose, and for the most part, they still do.

However, I found writing to be my comfort and escapism.

What I bring to this artistic expression is a look into flat Earth with a different spin and narrative from the mundane politically correct tripe and spiel regurgitated by the press and general public to the 'race card' cliche pulled out every time race is mentioned. In this book, I pull no punches and give a voice to what many of us think but are too scared to say. Hence the title, Your World, My Mind.

* Artwork done during incarceration

Chapter 1

THE VAGRANT

He lay there oblivious, ragged, malnourished.

No one seemed to care.

The emerald carpet his bed,

The moonlit canopy his roof,

His ashen face weathered,

Frozen feet hardened to a hoof.

You smelt him before you saw him,

Then came your offensive stare.

But he carried a donor card.

If you could only bear the fresh organs of a tramp.

Chapter 2

DO I LOVE YOU?

Do I love you?

Even though words of apology fail, my cuticle-pricked ears and the depravity of night stalks the furthest edges of day.

Under a bashful moon, how bewitching is your silhouetted beauty?

Flowing wine drowns out all inhibitions, while open fires demand a state of utter abandon.

Flared nostrils submerge in your sweet, scented sweat.

We entwine like electric eels. But am I the fish, or the fisherman?

We never argue in bed.

Agreeable minds have no need for an interpreter.

My heart is near to bursting.

Do I love you?

Puppies play with kittens,

Soldiers dance in the trenches,

Prenups are ripped to pieces,

Acrimony has no reason to rise.

My mouth quickens your panting breath.

Our hearts melody a viola's happy concerto.

Your cheeks are flushed with heats of red blusher,

Smudged lips locked like bloody leeches, kisses lubricating an already-saturated rose.

My affection knows no other garden and modesty has no hiding place.

Ankles, insides of wrists and backs of knees savored; your sweetness has left bees without industry.

Birds ever chirp at your song.

In passions nest, never has a poet plagiarized these words,

And still, you ask,

Do I love you?

Chapter 3

MISPLACED TRUST

My mother gave me to a white man named Miles from social services.

She said, "You're going to the park." But I asked, "Why the suitcases then?"

Her answer was stark.

I ended up being fostered by strangers and could not understand the betrayal as a five-year-old.

Then came the beast. I was violently abused by my dad.

The man who I knew the least.

He was supposed to protect me, but he was so angry.

I didn't see my mother for years, no one to comfort me,

No one to dry my tears or put my slippers back on when he hung me with my pissy sheets.

He said, "Beatings will straighten you out."

"I'm going to beat some sense into you, boy, or beat some out, a few licks never harmed anyone."

But wounds heal though my mind is permanently scarred,

Controlling my anger has been a struggle, forgiving has been so hard.

I grew up to beat bullies in the playground. The only fight I lost was in court.

I killed a man in my twenties; re-lived trauma of a sort.

Writing this song, I was so filled with pain I had to reinvent myself to hide the shame that I don't know how to love.

Chapter 4

THE ASYLUM SEEKER

Existing in the shadows of death,

In a land laid to waste,

I beheld her tribal tattooed pushtuned face.

A beautiful woman of slender structure,

Full cherry lips and dipping waist.

She grabbed me with her saddened eyes of crystal grey.

They chilled my very soul.

They whispered, "Rescue me from this grave of the living dead."

This pile of ashes destroyed by the red.

And forgotten antiquity of war.

Rescue me, oh, foreign face!

I will do your bidding unquestionably, beckon to your call.

No need to speak to me of love; just treat me well.

Oh, traveler, please rescue me from this hell.

Amnesty took me far and wide two years past,

Before I returned, my heart in apprehension burned.

I searched for her at her begging spot,

Outside the bombed-out butcher's shop.

Not sighting her, I began to dread,

Wondering if she were alive or dead.

Then by her swan like walk and Pushtun squawk,

I recognized my sultress.

Bewitched by her eyes of translucent grey,

Peeping through a torn dusty veil.

She whispered as I passed the queue:

"Oh, rescue me from these merciless mortars and guns,

These warring fathers and sons.

In this land of torture and poverty,

I ask not for dowry.

Only for a place to rest and peace of mind.

Oh, rescue me, foreign face, so kind."

Chapter 5

THE SQUARE'S TALE

I went to a party as a square,

An introvert with little flair,

But surprisingly made a friend there,

A charmer with such debonair.

I had a few drinks and let down my hair,

Came out of my shell but did not care.

I lost my virginity and dignity to cheer,

It was a champagne and cocaine affair.

I feel trapped in a bottle like a genie.

Surviving on drugs and drink,

In denial, I don't want to think.

If only my parents could see me,

Naked on a shag pile of dog ends,

Sharing a needle with my new friends.

I became so hyper, the orgy clown,

That's why he gave me a sedative to calm me down,

They call it 'brown.'

I felt so sick; I tried to call home,

But threw up all over the phone.

Since then, i've been hooked.

You could say in a word "f...ked."

My life's been hit by a quake,

The price paid not to be a party pooper.

I never dreamt I'd be such a loser.

Tricked by the piper, living like a rat,

Dancing to the purring of a cat,

Lord don't let me go out like that.

One more drink, one more toot,

Then i'll give this habit the boot.

Cross my heart and hope to kill a cop

If, after this promise, I do not stop.

Chapter 6

BEAUTIFUL WOMAN

When my voice begins to croak,

As happens, mere mortal folk.

Or nimble skip should lose its spring,

God forbid the very thing.

Will you love me still?

When weathered skin no longer clings,

Flesh-tight and luscious locks,

Streak misty white.

When milk teeth fail to sparkle bright,

Will you love me still?

When temptress eyes of tomorrow do bag,

And firm breasts surely southward sag.

When you've kissed the best days

That were had,

Will you love me still?

When my field is tilled to the peak,
Libido surrendering frail and weak.
When progeny I can flower no more,
And passion snubs my termite door,
Will you love me still?

When static is broken by aches and moans,
And death creeps in my aged bones,
When Gabriel scoops me in his quill,
Will you love me still?

Chapter 7

TEARS OF A FOOL

I lost my job and fell into debt,

You're the love that answered my call.

Picked me up when I would fall.

You could have had any man you chose,

But you stayed loyal even though I was broke.

You endured hard times like a suffragette,

Like when the gas was disconnected,

And jack frost bit at our toes.

I wasn't rejected.

Hot lovemaking helped us through the big freeze.

Baby, forgive me, please.

The way I treated you was so cruel,

These are the tears of a fool.

Even when the bailiffs came,

And reprocessed the plasma screen and new sofa,

I was sure it was over.

But you offered them your widowed mother's ring,

I was a pauper, but you made me your king.

I became abusive when I started to drink,

Your girlfriends' said.

For putting up with me,

You needed a shrink.

You had faith when I lost mine,

Baby, forgive me one more time.

Forgive me, please.

The way I treated you was so cruel,

These are the tears of a fool.

Things started looking better,

All of a sudden, I'm bringing in the doe.

But because it was dirty money,

You didn't want to know.

It broke your heart when I began to cheat,

I wish I told those other girls no.

Baby, please come home.

I've given up the hoes, the streets,

The bottle and the yayo.

Baby, forgive me, please.

The way you suffered was so cruel,

These are the tears of a fool.

Chapter 8

MY SON

"Everyone's a shotter or a rapper a Moncler jacket,

And a CP hat don't mek yu gangsta

A mic ah bad boy beat, an ah fat spliff and a beast rap don't mek yu ah gangsta

Real smooth a jack move an cocked Glot,

Yu saluted badness till your boy got shot

Yu barled murder, an ya muda dead from shock

Hounds vied for blood, war drums in the hood but I bet a vest never stopped a head top.

Come like everybody deh pan drugs!

So I shun road cos snitches bun code

An ah dem talk di business,

It's a rap,

Rats, cats, an human canaries

It's the same nationwide,

Though mugshots vary

An blood spill out like a bloody mary

But if you kill my son an I kill your son

How many Nubian stars must get bun under the blood clart sun

The clues in the lyrick

The battles pyrrhic, a wah di bloodclart du yu

Niga put yu on, but yu tief his plug,"

"Then bragged about it, how about it

You got lit up for the lack of love shown

Ya shit bag aint Gucci so you aint that smug yu little shitter could have been a real big hitter

Now yu just hate yu wack life and your waste man state

Selling 16s from a wheelchair as if your name was bait till yu got nabbed

Yu dashed weh yu gat… weak MFKR might as well a've put it in the feds dem lap

Scared like puss

I knew yu would flop nigga went QE an turned OP,

Sang so much the feds begged him to stop

4yrs concurrent surrounded by enemies,

Ya lifes done, needless to say your a son of a gun

But if you kill my son and I kill your son

How many Nubian sons must get bun

Under the bloodclart sun

The clues in the lyrick the battle is pyrrhic

A wah di bloodclart du yu"

Excerpt From: My Son. Apple Books.

Chapter 9
MISUNDERSTOOD

I'm stuck somewhere between stop and go,

High and low,

A tear and a smile,

Man, and a dependent child.

I'm a walking contradiction.

You remain an addiction so misunderstood.

Reality or fiction, you're an angel, you're a vixen,

Swirling in my blood.

Swirling in my blood.

I'm suspended between Hades and Heaven,

Thirteen and seven.

A rapid heartbeat from death.

I fell asleep in a poppy field,

And woke to a dragon's breath.

Scorched, I jumped into an ocean of glue,

Got washed up on a magic mushroom.

I've got to get away from you,

Got to get away from you.

I'm a walking contradiction.

You remain an addiction so misunderstood.

Reality or fiction, you're an angel, you're a vixen,

Swirling in my blood.

Swirling in my blood.

I abseil high rises in a rocked-out city,

And ski cold streets of snow.

Neon lights are blinding. I stumble in the glare,

Such a beautiful glow.

Northern lights flashing in a purple haze sky,

As sad and strange faces pass me by

There's a familiar body on a pissed stained bed,

I'm freaked out because it looks like me.

But I'm high on the ceiling,

Without care or feeling, so how could it be?

I'm a walking contradiction.

You remain an addiction so misunderstood.

Reality or fiction, you're an angel, you're a vixen,

Swirling in my blood.

Swirling in my blood.

Chapter 10

THE DARK SIDE OF LOVE

She glowed in the moonlight even when entertaining other men,

Rain turns to mist, then fades slowly, like a bad memory.

My chest swells when I remember her.

Some call it growing pains.

I named her Sparkle because that's what she did.

Her body killed her dress; her buttocks swallowed her thong,

Street lamps accentuated her curves like a film star.

Men fell at her feet.

She was as beautiful as fire, burning the willing,

I'll forever carry the luggage of that first night.

She made love hearts out of spliff smoke as I fell into her man-trap

Gin-scented those seducing lips,

Her skin felt invitingly warm; her heart was cold.

Love making was an out-of-body experience,

Sparkle had daddy issue and i looked just like him!

Her smile stopped traffic,

A stranger once described a black aura around her;

Though he was color blind.

Forgive me if I go on; have you ever been in love?

Girls hated her; she juggled hearts, apparently even theirs.

Sometimes she would finish my sentences,

Or the last morsel on my plate and drinks too, I didn't mind.

After consuming my heart, what else was left?

Lies were syrup dripping off her tongue,

Mother believed Sparkle's violet eyes, ebony skin,

And red hair was the Devil's creation.

She took me to hell so many times I thought I was home.

I bought her everything she wanted; my soul was free,

I'm still paying the interest.

A postcard came with a photo of her pregnant,

The man hugging her was her cousin?

She needed money for an abortion.

But decided to have the child.

I can't see it, but friends say it looks just like him.

The boy is striking; no doubt he'll grow to be a heartbreaker.

Chapter 11

MR BELLYFULL

I an I love mi food

Conks an lobster get

Mi ina di mood

But nah let mi get rude

Cha,,, bring the menu

Time fi arda..

Fi mi starter, tink i'll have

Sum cheese an bun

Den a bowl of cornmeal

Porridge wid a hint of cinna-mon

Next gimi a generous piece

Of Ginger cake an a glarss

Of rum, mek a list:

Karrat juice, coconut drops, barnana Fritters

And one, Guiness punch to wash down mi lunch

Waiter, waiter, wa mek you tek so Long?

Mi ready for the mein carse

An hungry na rarse

Bring couple a fri dumpling

And a Snapper fish

A wa happen to dat deh dish?

It look like Vincent Price dead twice

Yuh nah get full price!

Hear wah, gimmi de curry goat an rice

Nyam, cut swalla

Waiter, a wa di debt...

Kiss mi neck, mi yam already

And mi wallet foget!

"Sorry sa, i'll have to call the manager."

Fi manage who?

'Bring im cum,

"Hello, a problem paying you'll just have to wash plates."

'A who yu a talk?

Come like

Yu tek bad man fi knife an fork,

Yu na si oww, di Snapper cole

And the bun it ole

Yu car si di fly inna di bottom

Of di duty bowl?

Any how, di rice, was fresh?

All now mi car digest.

'Oscar, call the police

Eh,eh, yu muss tink yu ah deal wid bad man neice

Fossy, le gu mi coller

A jesta yu a jesta

Mi a di food inspector member!

And as for yu Jerk chicken

Mi si all rat a yam dat

Inna di kichen

So shut ya mout ya trets dem holla

Fix up fossy

Si yu same time tomarra

[Rarse Jamaican slang for buttocks/ arse.

Fossy /Fool A Derogatory term]

Chapter 12

GRANDAD WINT

He was funny, kind, and attentive.

He fixed my tie and picked my fro with pride,

So full of love was he, you felt his warmth inside.

The trees bow in sorrow; the sea holds back the tide,

And I wept under the Weeping willow,

The day my Grandad died.

I danced the Merengue with him and ate out of his plate,

But the Lord called him back too soon, for heaven could not wait.

Though you'll always be close to me, be it in your sleepy state.

He defeated me in combat, a warrior through and through,

And the skill of champions, great man, I acquired it all from you.

He had a tash and such panache.

I wanted to be just like him.

But when asked if I'd used his shaver,

I'm ashamed to admit I lied.

He said, "Time will tell young whiskers."

Now I'm a slave to the razor.

Itching, Im tested, and I'm tried

The trees bow in sorrow; the sea holds back the tide,

And I wept under the weeping willow,

The day my granddad died.

My heart hummed a happy tune.

As I cuddled like a cub between you and Gran,

Listening to Ken Boothe sing 'Everything I Own,'

Upon the Goodman gram,

You brought me clothes and spoiled me,

Giving up your last pound.

Granddad, you're surely missed,

Our hearts are forever bound.

The trees bow in sorrow; the sea holds back the tide,

And I wept under the weeping willow,

The day my Grandad died.

Chapter 13

MUMMY WINT

Dark cherry smile, beautiful and mild.

A matriarch of heart-filled care,

Outspoken, soft, but always fair.

Gentle in her demeanor but tough if provoked,

She was an apron to her family and to her husband, a cloak. Mummy Wint.

My second mom, she had eyes to see the hidden world, righteous to the core.

I never heard her swear nor saw her wrong any soul

When I hurt myself, we would kick down the offending obstruction, be it a wall, fence, or bush,

She fed the hungry, quenched the thirsty and trampled on the adder in the brush.

Nerissa Wint, the mother of mothers.

When me and grandad would spar,

She was the referee that saved me when I caught a right hook.

She was a brilliant baker and also a fabulous cook.

And if I did anything untoward, proverbs rolled off her tongue, morality and principles were the armor that kept her family strong.

Hugs and kisses her shield.

She is with Allah now,

Her faith and book are sealed.

Yet we are at your heels.

Beloved, gran Nerissa Wint.

Chapter 14

NERISSA WINT

My dearest Gran, was a legacy of righteousness.

A committed mother and Allah-fearing anchor of goodness,

Witnessed whether you say Illah or Yahweh,

A studious and religious theologian,

She enquired about the Koran and painfully explained the contradictions in the Bible.

She begged for the light, an honor I undertook.

She said, "Do not tell Grandad." But eventually, he found the noble book and threatened to throw it onto the road.

"I said, "One, you are my heart, and two, this is your respected abode."

Allah will defend what I can not. His relenting told me he, too, had doubts.

Me and gran shared a secret, and now the truth was out,

For I read the Bible to her every morning, slept many nights in her room, and questioned her and grandad, Even the pastors in the church got caught in the fray,

Fast forward thirty five years, what else can i say,

On the last day of her life, she said she was stuck in the mud

And pleaded with my sister and her son to pray in the Islamic way

And took her shahada under her eldest son's request,

And so died a purified Muslim and Allah does know best.

Chapter 15

KIDS

What would a child be without a mucky face?

Curious eyes, so surprised

A cheeky smile

Or streaming tears

A runny nose

Spontaneous thought

Bad behavior

A forgiving nature

Stamping feet

Clumsy walk

Gibberish talk

Questions, "Why?"

And "Please, can I...?"

A little white lie.

"It wasn't me!"

What would a child be without understanding?

Chapter 16

GRIME

The ALF lost Dolly the sheep.

Butchers sell poisoned meat,

Recipe for murder, check ya burger.

GM fries and get wise.

Digestive systems under attack,

CJD remains a fact.

Herbivores made carnivores cause,

Friends of the Earth burnt down the stores.

Organic for the rich, pesticides kill the poor,

This is a class war draw!

Dial tone; location blown,

Kid, get off that mobile phone,

Microwaves radiate your dome.

Cell damage and tumors heed the rumors,

Robo cops and cyborg troopers.

I spy great pie-in-the-sky satellites,

Ain't just for human tracking.

It's mind control with government backing,

Hence the high pitch ringing in ya ears,

Enough to reduce a grown man to tears.

Caught in the World Wide Web, have no fear.

Here you shall find,

Lyrics to educate and liberate your mind.

Nod ya head but do not whine,

There's a new meaning to grime.

If conspiracy theories are for the eccentric,

Why facial scanners and biometrics?

The erosion of liberties tell ya brays,

No cash bar-coding within ten years.

The beast controls the worlds bank,

Thoughts of a think tank.

Cranks say it's for the public good,

Like female hormones in water and food.

Destroying fertility by sterility,

Baby boys changing gender.

Welcome to the age of the gender bender,

Don't wanna spook ya.

Just remember,

There are pcbs in the food chain,

And E numbers that'll fry ya brain.

That's why they lock up the Vimto generation,

And feed ya kids Prozac,

While Harry and Hue Blair chilled at number10

And smoked crack, not even an ASBO.

Well, here you shall find,

Lyrics to educate & liberate ya mind.

Nod ya head but do not whine,

There's a new meaning to grime.

It's an open prison your tagged,

So, pull up ya jeans, and drop ya swag.

Ya heads in a spin

Chip n' pin.

The data's loading,

Ya cold and blue; check ya serotonin,

You may be a child of gene cloning.

Programmed through ya neurotransmitter,

Hearing voices; they've made you bitter.

Listen! Critter ya,

Just one of a litter of ice babies,

Born of dead man's sperm.

Carrying corpse flu, sad but true.

Scientists fail to learn from the aids virus,

Dissecting folks like Set did Osiris.

We walk the plank of death, IVF.

In an ocean of darkness, no rescue ship.

Waiting mothers having daughter's child,

I heard them debating on a talk show,

Incest by insemination,

A violation of principles;

Sacred and ancient.

The end is nigh; my final statement.

Here you shall find,

Lyrics to educate and liberate ya mind.

Nod ya head but do not whine,

Cos there's a new meaning to grime.

*Written in 2003-5

Chapter 17

A SAD AFFAIR

Without reprieve, the end is nigh,

The undoing of creations, my alibi.

Thread the planets on a rainbow like a necklace,

Gather the cotton clouds and lay them down.

Uproot the trees, place them in single file,

Stack the Earth in a neat, tidy pile.

Unplug the sea and unhook the sun.

Kiss me, for my heart is done.

Pick every fruit before full bloom.

Roll up space and cover the moon.

Call the angels from up high.

Hang the dew grass out to dry.

Level the mountains and cluster the stars.

Free anguished hearts from guilt's chains'n'bars.

Collect the insects, pen the animals.

Archive all songs, proverbs, and parables.

Net the fish, cage the birds,

Then line up all skeptics to hear these words:

"I testify my love."

Chapter 18

MY SHAME

My mother never calls my fathers name

But when she's mad apparently I'm just like him.

Every month he sends provisions from his store

I think she loves to hate him

My aunt said, she bathed me a dozen times;

To remove his smell, then handed me over

It took six months for her to hold me again

Actually I'm a failed abortion.

They inter married once, Muslims and Christians.

He hid my mother in the cellar, for several months

When the army came, when they found her;

She had fresh love bites and bruised thighs

If she screamed she would have been detected

"A fifteen year old girl must be lying" they said.

Mostly its honour protected not reputation

Uncle says it would have been better if she had died

Grandmother can't see me, but she's not blind

No body will give me there daughter's hand

"I smell like a Serb"

Anti depressants make Bosnia a happy memory.

Poppies are her favourite flower,

Opium makes his slave forget

I think she hates to love him

Chapter 19

ASKING FOR FORGIVENESS

This world's an open prison; i've died a thousand times.

Surrounded by darkness, I'm buried alive.

I'm asking for forgiveness. Why does that seem strange?

Lord, i've seen the light, but only you feel my pain.

And the Lord said, "Let all repentant sinners come unto me."

And he offered me an olive branch under the sycamore tree.

I was filled with joy, that sweet joy of reprieve.

But what will it take beloveds to make others believe?

See, the wise learn from the mistakes of others, and fools learn on their own.

The Devil is defeated here,

Let the wretch come home.

Now it's more than I deserve, so I thank you for your time.

Seems expressions of the heart can ease a troubled mind.

And I'm so sorry, so sorry,

Sorry, I stole... I'm sorry I lied.

My daddy was a good man,

And mama, she tried.

I became a fish to devil's water,

Neglected my daughter and my son.

Was addicted to getting high and settled drama with the gun.

A lover of loose women... I broke every heart I touched.

Came to jail for my sins... The Lord deemed them too much.

My heart was so hard; they didn't believe me when I cried.

But haven't you seen the caterpillar become a butterfly?

All things change, so why can't I?

I'm asking for forgiveness. Why does that seem strange?

Lord, i've seen the light, but only you feel my pain.

So don't call me Barabas, no!

Call me by my name; I'm a servant of the Lord, why should I be ashamed?

If bitterness devours the owner's heart, what have we gained?

I'm asking for forgiveness. Why does that seem strange?

Lord, i've seen the light, but only you feel my pain.

Chapter 20

TRUTH LOCKED DOWN

Truth locked down.

Behind my fiberglass parasitic-filled masks,

I thought, why are there 74 patented variants of covid registered before 2016?

DNA-changing technology, not quite a vaccine,

Yes, humans, you are the new guinea pigs it seems.

Monkeypocks, arrhythmia, and shingles are minor side effects.

Heart attacks and death are fobbed off as unknown irritants, even if they never showed symptoms before.

So, if you catch a cold, don't sneeze too hard.

Or stand under a 5G mast, or you'll be tagged and bagged quicker than you can scream

Gates or Fauci, who are you calling conspiracy theorists, are you daft?

Chapter 21

FALSEHOOD

False-hood is one word with two halves, like a snake's tongue.

Like a backbiter with two faces whose handshake is firm when greeting friends,

But whose slanderous words can end marriages, break bonds, and destroy nations.

Chapter 22

THE MELANATED JOURNEY - THE DARK WOMB

From the day we were created

Beings most hated

a victim of genocide the devil he celebrated

born on a full moon

death was in the air

the birds sung a strange tune...

lightning flashed

are third eye smashed

and blood rained like a monsoon...

i said doom gloom

let the melanated journey dark womb

i put you in the picture no need to assume

the devil became man's closest friend nothing would ever be the same again, see the curtain of mercy has been drawn brothers-the antichrist is born...

Dameon chuckled an cackled with his howling mother the jackal

israel broke the covenant loosing the sanctuary of the tabernacle...

Crusades kissed goodbye to the Grail in battle... but came back to heard us on ships like cattle...

from the west they came withn curse of cain

from the land of Nod

good god... I said

Doom gloom

let the malenated journey the dark womb

I put you in the picture no need to assume.

chiefs sought power from talismans an witches to for fill their unbless wishes...

since Nimrod we bare the wrath of god for the sins of our nation

nubians flogged Garvey sobbed for are plight an sufferation

The two edge sword shall bring justice in the next duaration....

we bare the curse for now it gets worse...

Locust swept... farmers in debt... angles wept chaos has crept from the place it once slept..

tonadoes hurricanes

an famine... imagine, blood

sweat tears an pain the devils reign

take another terror trip the atombs now split...

Gog an Magog finally met and went to war...

We witness catastrophes... like never before... women weep for the secret in their womb...

the new born are fed reactive waste on a silver spoon, no hope, false hope

In the absence of god pagans crowned a man pope

renegades of Rome couldn't cope... they conspired treason marrying the idea to elope

they hung from the highest branch by rope... Doom gloom...

Iet the malenated journey the dark womb

i put you in the picture no need to assume.

the all seeing eye- watched from afar... while metorites fell to earth like a shooting stars

the fortunate fled to the east but even there they bowed to the beast selling their faith for a small price

while pope ate the flesh an drank the blood of Jesus christ... an yu feel seh im nice..

leaders escaped to basses in space but found their no protection or resting place...

the trumpet of the lord was sounded armies of darkness surrounded...

jinn and men suffered the same fate for their evil spree of torture an hate.

I said doom gloom...

let the melanated journey the dark womb

I put you in the picture no need to assume.

Chapter 23

TIDA

She's so sweet, funny, and petite.

She's untouchable, intangible, and unique.

I yearn for a meeting, but her heart is fleeting,

If the sun doesn't shine, it's because she isn't mine.

Oh, Tidy Tida the catwalk queen,

Africa's jewel,

I'm her plaything, a willing fool, and I am falling.

In front or behind the camera, she's so precise, like a sniper.

Her angles defy shutter speed.

She's an artist in motion.

Cut from designer cloth,

A marvelous marvel, indeed.

Africa's jewel,

I'm her plaything, a willing fool, and I'm falling a fool for heartbreak.

Chapter 24

BOURNEMOUTH

A single red rose obscured by a thousand floral hearts,

Who said the world is void of love?

A smile, a nod of acknowledgment, yet you snub me.

I came across your beautiful countenance on social media.

If I messaged you, would it be a step too far?

How do strangers remove the barrier of estrangement?

I observe you at the bus stop, come rain or shine,

A shower of flattery fails to make you mine.

How do strangers overcome the barrier of estrangement?

My efforts are met with frowns.

A love boat off the Bournemouth coast has run aground,

A sea of tears, I have no raft!

If you only talk to me, I know we could be friends.

On top of these Boscombe cliffs, a starling chick hatches

One life begins as another one ends.

Chapter 25

DON'T CUT ME

Fluid movement of Somali hips

Shapes shifting, tocking, locking,

Big bums bouncing to the Niko-based beat.

Guddaa Guddaa Guddaa Guddaa.

My Mogadishu cousin thinks it's her sister's engagement.

In my beautiful Puntland, myrrh danced in the warm breeze,

Treetops caressed the soft wings of hummingbirds.

Guddaa Guddaa Guddaa Guddaa.

Cardamom Kahwa quenched the thirst while tef sweetened my lips,

This was before my first bridal kiss; then innocence was bliss and flat-chested.

Guddaa Guddaa Guddaa Guddaa.

My black curls rested on delicate shoulders.

No niqāb, veils didn't suit pretty girls. Ruddish skin caught the blazing sun.

Daddy passed his pipe and chuckled when I coughed,

Then made me sip spicy coffee.

One inconspicuous smiley aunt,

Called me to help her carry a goat-skinned mat.

The door slammed behind me.

I was grabbed, gagged, then laid flat.

A fat lady sat on top of me, holding my arms.

I tried to kick till my mom hushed me, gesturing a slap.

My skinny legs were tied like a young gazelle.

I felt pain in my stomach; my eyes rolled back as they stole

My future, joy, womanhood, and trust

When I came round, two ugly witches were tying cloth over my stitches.

Not only the moon cried blood that night.

How could I ever forget Hagessa?

Guddaa Gudaa Guddaa Guddaa, never!

Chapter 26

DEVIL SHIP

Tell me, Mandingo, about the devil ship,

And how many Africans escaped the hell-mans whip.

Tell me of the slaves bleeding, cut, and raw,

And how many ancestors met the angels at the oar.

Tell me of the warrior who broke the red-faced captain's neck,

Then took the cannon underarm, blowing a hole in the lower deck.

Remind me how many mutineers were saved by drift

Wood and plank,

And the tears of joy shed when the Willie Lynch sank.

Tell me, grandfather, can it be true that brave Mandingo

Was none other but you?

Chapter 27

MISSING

A pale explorer entered the village of the Watusi tribe,

While a buoyant chief sat amongst his people in colorful pride.

The insolent stranger snapped his royal image.

To much surprise, on carbon did his soul materialize.

Juju men were dazzled by the white man's magic.

From awe came suspicion, then panic.

The chief, in all the excitement became ill

Not to find a cure in herb or bitter pill.

Screams of foul play reached fever pitch,

Justice was demanded by every shaman charlatan and witch.

The ghost-faced photographer was buried alive in shock

With a camera, diary, mirror, and clock.

And the murdered chief's portrait

Hung upon the palace wall,

His spirit trapped for all eternity.

Chapter 28

MADAGASCAN GIRL

Her cheeks were two halves of a blemishless peach,

The moon mirrored her mesmerizing face,

Her saffron hair shoulder length yet out of reach.

Her eyes are stars that defied the night,

Her lips, a puckered rose with its fragrant delight.

Her ears heard no malice, and tongue spoke nothing crude.

Her pleasantries are tangible,

Her warm temperament sets the mood.

Aicha's grace is that of a swan upon a rippling lake,

Why all hearts swim to pursue her as a monogamous mate

Chapter 29

TOP HAT AND TAILS

Knock the smug couple off the cake,

Burn the confetti,

Melt the ugly ice swan.

You've been stood up at the alter my boy,

But life goes on.

Cork the wine,

Consume the roses in fire

There's no love,

Cupid's a little liar.

Blow out the candles,

Drown your sorrows,

Break the fancy plates.

Insult your in-laws,

And dis' your mates.

Holler out of tune while the band looks on,

Aphrodite's a fraud,

Her love's a con.

And when you're certain you've done your worst,

Apologize to the bride for your foolish outburst.

For heaven's sake, she was only late.

An honest mistake.

Prat!

Chapter 30

DOUBLE HARVEST

If spring ne'er smiled upon the cold,

Then winter nights would freeze the mold.

Nor panting breath to thaw the bone,

Nor maids apron be an upward throne.

Farmers' sickle burns in idle hand,

While weeds and thorns overtake the land.

Shepherd eloped with fair delight,

The wolves and sheep have taken flight.

Millstone has not since kissed the corn,

But harvest child has yet to be born.

Maids' churns not played its butt'ry beat,

Dry rye, her father's crusty treat.

Elopers with babe have come to plead,

Forgiveness for their unblessed seed.

With gifts of ox and coat of fox,

And pipes tied neatly in a box.

For son has proved a handsome mate,

And wedding's set for the harvest date.

The land is tilled, the larders filled,

The dowry paid; grandfather's thrilled.

Chapter 31

ASSIMILATION

If she straightened her hair,

Wore blue contacts and lightened her skin,

De-plumped her arse and bent her back,

Deflated her lips,

Lipo-sucked her hips.

Broke the rhythm of her steps,

Had two left feet when she danced or crept,

Flicked the chip from her shoulder,

Ate bland food and laughed less loud,

Would you say her assimilation has made you more proud?

If I kept my hands at my side when speaking, with passion

So as not to be a disturbance to your uncultured crowd.

If I shunned my race,

And walked alone so as not to be deemed a thug or member of a gang.

If I pulled up my pants and dressed in your fashion,

And listened to the type of soulless music that I can't stand.

If I changed my religion, married your progeny,

And embraced your history with pride,

Would you then say I had integrated?

And accept the truth your heart has denied

Chapter 32

LOST FOR WORDS

Who can stop the war machine from mowing down our homes,

Wounding our flesh and breaking our bones,

Destroying our fields and making us refugees?

Who will hear the cries of my mother when she pleads,

"Pharaoh, don't kill my baby, don't kill my baby please?"

I have a library of words but don't know where to start,

What do you say to a world with a rotten heart?

While we turn the other cheek, to whom shall we protest?

Politicians are demons, and the devil owns the press.

How can we trust foreign policy when you sponsor brutality and call the oppressors friend?

You say you work for peace, but we know you just pretend.

I can't keep silent about these atrocities, but where do I begin?

Genocide's a crime, but suicide's a sin,

I have a library of words but don't know where to start.

What do you say to a world with a rotten heart?

In the face of tyranny, what's the terrorized to do?

Global tyranny, but who's terrorizing who?

I have a library of words but don't know where to start,

What do you say to a world with a rotten heart?

Chapter 33

HEARTS & MINDS

Roll up enlist, Jerry throw ya dice.

What ya got to lose,

But ya kiss ass life?

Tom, don't forget ya hard hat,

Metal jacket, and boots.

Bring ya own gun.

Attention, all recruits.

Chemical Ali created a blast,

While the Mahdi Army defended Najaf,

The sunnies hit the green belt

And caused a blood bath.

Insurgents led by Zarqawi,

Left so many dead.

They call it death valley.

Mayday, Mayday, Ricochet

Ten marines injured and three killed

Saddam's sons went out in a blaze of glory

Faces all shot up the footage was gory.

Comical Ali and General Powell got pally,

No laughing matter this is death valley

Rockets hit Al-Jazeera for giving a voice to terrorists,

Now the so-called liberators are targeting journalists.

War protesters marched and signed a petition,

To stop civil kidnap, waterboarding and rendition,

Torture and the use of white phosphorus.

Public opinion is what it cost us.

Soldiers in porn gate, swear official collusion

Sexual abuse an electrocution.

Sold by Perv's Dot Com Distribution.

Chenie watched the preview with bush and rice.

The ménage á trois were so shocking.

They watched it twice.

False limbs guide dogs and shades,

ID tags, body bags, and spades.

Remember, kids in Iraq throw hand grenades.

To date, an uncountable number of lives lost.

Orders from the top,

The insurgency must stop.

Bomb the newlyweds, do what you have to do

Tell the press terrorists have weddings too.

Run run kids evade capture.

They're killing Muslims in Halabja,

Here comes the reconnaissance

Don't let them catch ya,

If ya a tuff nut, G.I. Lin will crack ya.

Sumara, fifty gunships enter the drama,

Militants out to lunch, next stop Fallujah

Bring ya own gas masks.

A.K.S. and armor.

When shit hits the fan,

You'll need an embalmer.

Don't forget your Prozac.

They'll keep ya calm from shooting up ya veins and self-harm.

Halliburton hired trucks,

Evergreen containers, and private pick-ups,

With so much cash to steal

They didn't want a hick-up.

They smuggled artifacts bodies and cash over the border,

Theft and kidnap is the new world order.

It's the reign of the beast.

They'll probably put one in my nut when this gets released.

False limbs, guide dogs, and shades,

ID tags, body bags, and spades.

Remember, kids in Iraq throw hand grenades.

*This was written in 2003

Chapter 34

HOW ARE YOU GONNA GET OUT OF THIS ONE?

Do you know what it's like to be a nigger at night?

A walk on the damn streets at night,

Less you hear the sirens and see the blue lights.

You getting stopped, searched, and cuffed tight.

A good ass-kicking, not a witness in sight, brought before the judge all the faces are white.

So, excuse me, your honor, if I seem uptight, spitting and cussing like I do on the mic.

I am just a little pissed off, right?

So you look in the jury, what have you got? Six undercover racists and half a dozen cops

Plus, ya defense doesn't look too hot; you realize too late that their part of the plot,

Now you feel like you just got shot.

So, tell me, how ya gonna get out of dis one nigger?

Jump the dock and fist one.

Maybe throw a couple of rights and miss one.

Time's running out, don't take too long.

There was a struggle, and a wrought nigger broke out of court and just made a crime report.

Shoot on sight policy's death for short damn nigger better not get caught,

Now he's hungry like a mutha two days on the run

So held up Kentucky with a loaded gun.

I know where the hell him he get that from?

Guess he must have got it from the cop he chinned, before he dropped, flipped, and spinned.

Seem n..ger been working in the gym, right?

But now, no doubt, he's out on a limb, so he robbed a crack house for cash like Bolt on speed.

He made a sixty-yard dash but still caught two in the ass.

Hopping, dropping, losing blood fast.

Armed response caught sight and gave chase.

Last thing he heard before they shot him in the face was,

"How ya gonna get out of dis one n..ger?"

Jump the dock and fist one.

Maybe throw a couple of rights and miss one.

Time's running out, don't take too long.

It's touch and go.

You gotta feel it for a bruda.

Breathing through a tube not recognized by his mother.

Nigger's a survivor.

He might just pull through, but he faces ten to life if he do

N..ger gonna die, that's what you thought.

But n..ger survived, n..ger back in court.

Oh, you of little faith.

Public and press came to hear the case, cops at the ready with gats and mace.

He got ten years sectioned as basket-case

Blame the system, mutha f.ker.

Don't blame the race,

For the injustice faced in this redneck place.

And tell me, how you gonna get outer this one n..ger?

Jump the dock and fist one.

Maybe throw a couple of rights and miss one.

Time's running out, don't take too long.

Chapter 35

ORPHANS FOR DIAMONDS

On the road, limbs piled up like black ivory set the mood.

This is the jungle.

It could be anywhere in Africa,

But to the victims it is Eden, turned to hell.

Mortars can be heard nonstop; guns rattle like snakes.

In the belly button of the world, a roach sits smugly on his shrapnel throne.

Above, a farmer surveys his scorched plantation.

Last night, felled trees splintered like fleeing shadows,

Jackals and vultures are fattened here.

A one-eyed boy checks his cloth ball's rhythm against the boards of an abandoned shack.

Through whistling reeds, two bush rats scurry with all their belongings in their mandibles.

On the roadside, an armless child dreams of tying her laces, yet war will not leave peace alone.

Chapter 36

TATTOOS OF A BEDOUIN

Black memories of a Berber.

Medieval castles of broken teeth.

Dried oasis of tearful grief.

Rustic dust, powders, blood-stained swords,

Battered armor of sultans and lords.

Archenemies that share the same graves,

Legends of martyrs, brave.

Widowed souls wail behind a veil for lost love,

To be reunited in the paradise above.

Footprints of charcoal moors have blown away,

Though songs in the midnight dunes haunt the day.

Chapter 37

FEATHERED FRIENDS

As she flew away with him, the sun cracked,

And the Earth cooled,

I feel like the king of fools.

These cold days are my Arctic bane,

Torment the tundra of my mind.

I have little need for direction.

Sunsets were the compass to her heart.

Overhead an opportunist magpie

Overlooks sweet sorrow.

From his autonomy of twigs,

Frost has ruined my plumage.

Winter could do with a lick of paint,

Unkempt, I wallow in self-pity, but life goes on.

Who cares?

Chapter 38

A WORD TO YOUNG GIRLS

Poor single mother,

Her scuffed shoes have holes.

She's lonely,

And fed up with wearing old clothes.

Her bed sits damp, but only God knows if they'll cut her off before she pays the bill,

A bag of nerves, the stress is making her ill.

The world over.

The child knows best,

Till they flap their wings too early,

And fall from the nest.

Who said the wise learn from the mistakes of fools?

I guess someone must have changed the rules.

The baby won't stop crying; dad's on the run,

And he doesn't even know she's had his son.

Things were supposed to be rosy,

Strawberries and cream,

Being a teenage mother wasn't quite the dream.

Poor thing.

Her friends think she's mad,

For getting knocked up so soon,

Because she only turned sixteen in June.

These are words all young girls should know,

If a cute boy looks fly and good to go,

Remember these words,

And just say no.

N.O. spells no.

Kaz changes dirty nappies,

And breastfeeds like a milking cow.

Her delicate breasts have lost their shape now.

She's always tired and on the verge of tears,

One night without protection stole her golden years.

The world's over.

The child knows best,

Till they flap their wings too early,

And fall from the nest.

Who said the wise learn from the mistakes of fools?

I guess someone must have changed the rules.

She said she'll pick up the pieces,

When boo boo's two or three,

If she can find a college with a nursery.

When that time comes, she'll cross that bridge,

Meanwhile, they just cut her electric

The food has gone bad in the fridge.

For her to hold it together,

Takes fortitude and courage.

These are words all young girls should know.

If a cute boy looks fly and good to go,

Remember these words,

And just say no.

N.O. spells no.

Chapter 39

AFRICA'S HOLOCAUST

Oh when they came, the stop of the heart, the drop of the drum

Women fainted their limbs fell numb

Some fought in vain while others did run

From the ghost faced pirates who came to snatch, mother from daughter

And father from son.

They raped pillaged, burnt down the village, before dragging us to their vessels of doom

Beaten shackled, bleeding bruised, kicking screaming dazed confused

Chains cutting and rattling in the whole that stank

Profiteers of our tears… Lloyds of London, Thomas cook and Barclays bank

Vomit and pissed washed our septic wounds, suffocation by defecation

We prayed they would throw us overboard,, like their infected cargo, who sleep in watery graves

Those beautiful black dead-lucky slaves

The dock the bay, the cold display, the tar and branding, and come what may

The weighing, the flogging, the checking the batched

Paired from breeding, the strongest matched

Families forced to perform incestuous acts like beast upon the plain

The horror the guilt shush… the unspoken shame

Fields of malnourished children picking cotton ,or chopping cane,

Slave labor that built England, America, Portugal, France, and Spain.

And killed the indigenous tribes of the cari-be-ain.

One hundred million Africans were murdered or displaced.

Over four hundred years,

A sea of flesh, blood, and tears.

No reparations, no apology.

The final insult, no law was broken at the time,

To commit such genocide, back then, was fine…

Apparently.

Chapter 40

CALAA BAAJ

If I were a bird, I'd be a wild hawk, blacker than ravens night

I would soar to Hindustan and make a nest of saffron and the most fragrant jasmine,

And place in it the most colorful pearls, plucked from India's darkest ocean.

I would peer down from the peaks of the Himalayas, where I'd fish in its lakes and silvery pools.

I'll dry my wings in the wind and write freedom in its jet streams.

I'd tweet a song over Delhi and wash in the Ganges,

After basking in Rajasthan, I'd flutter off again to ancient Harappa

And Mohenjo Daro, where I'd contemplate our lost civilizations of the Dravidians

But as a Dalit who is touched by dreams,

I and my aspirations are untouchable, it seems.

Chapter 41

MARTIAN INQUISITION

Do not all mortals fear the darkness from whence they came?

Where not all men migrants from Africa; to the land they now so eagerly claim.

Are not all children unaware of race when they happily play?

Did you have a passport or visa in your hand at birth?

I hasten to ask, who holds the deeds to this priceless Earth,

Where seas and mountains are the only true borders where uncorrupted hearts have worth?

Do birds patrol the skies, or fish police the oceans?

Is hate not the foreigner that stirs your evil emotions?

Did you order black or white skin before your conception?

If so, these questions are also alien.

Chapter 42

SHANTY TOWN

I sit on an upturned bin inhaling glue,

On top of the tip where I live.

They call me a feral child, a born outcast

This is my ghetto

What else do I have to compare it to?

Am I a deprived child in a dark place in a pale man's world?

Inside my bag, everything's gray,

Life was a trip until they showed me how you live.

Chapter 43

FICKLE

My first love was an english bird who never cooked,

She lived on tea toast and coffee.

Her name was Finch.

She made lovely expressos with caramel, or was it honey?

Maybe it's a memory of a memory.

The day we separated; she called me a black bastard.

I thought her jewels for food were a fair exchange.

Would she have abhorred me less, knowing she saved me from hunger?

The next girl who referred to me with disdain was Spanish,

I left her for having an affair, which after more than a decade,

I learned was a lie.

I tried to repair the damage, but time doesn't extinguish such racist anger

Her tongue is still full of pain; her heart blacker than I,

My new lady is a Nigerian judge who gives my head no peace sentiments no justice and my manhood hard labour in the bedroom

She's mixed race,

I suppose it's the best of both worlds.

Chapter 44

LET ME REIGN

I am beauty's vapor yet formless, a mysterious mist hanging in the ether lighter than a feather,

Laden with tears,

I am heavier than your burden, though children rejoice in my,

Past, present, and future years,

I am gray, white, black, and blue; at other times, I take my color from the sunlight's ever-changing hue.

I am alone yet surrounded by a trillion droplets,

Let me rain, and I will replenish vegetation, fruits, and cattle.

But I can not quench mankind's thirst for blood,

Ironically, I am a whirlwind most devastating in battle.

I am wild and free.

But catch me if you can,

Let me reign.

Chapter 45

ONCE YOU HAD ME

Once you had me,

Before the dawn wiped serenity from the sun's sleepy eye

And love cursed the morn that swallowed my night.

Once passion's sheets were a tangle of flames, condensation dripped off the windows

Our bed has since imploded like a small universe,

Breathless clouds empty their icy cheeks

A hail of tears pelted heaven

Once you had me.

Your heartbeats in my bosom

Log fires have become embers

Weeping willows have dried, the homeless stir

Working girls sing to forget their integrity.

Gift of the gab failed my words,

A soup of letters lost in translation

Romantic sunsets were not picturesque enough to save us,

Wild pigs piss on truffles

Torrents flush lilies from flooded hills

Your strokes were like Piccaso's brush,

Once you had me.

My canvas was ripped from affection's easel,

I am the suffocating vine hanging around life;

Did I want too much?

I need to feel you.

The consolation is pain

Your eyes are flashes of light

Your voice, the wind that speaks to me, even in thunder.

Everything happens in cycles

Spiders crochet the dusky leaves

Children retire from play,

The fragrance of cooking pots torments vacant bellies

Little girls believe in fairies;

God forbid the day they discover heartbreak.

I sleep better in your shirt; they match your shorts.

Your toothbrush tastes of fresh kisses,

I pinch myself where you kissed me

Your shoes are too big to fill.

The dog sits by the door; tail wagging,

You are the world, everything is possible.

I read the future in yesterday's stars,

The old cherry tree is blossoming again, to all things they own season

When you come home it will be as if you never left,

Then I will reiterate love's refrain,

Once you had me.

CONCLUSION

Find here no rules, except for artistic license

Random as well as thoughtful expression.

My belief is that I'm here for a reason, as a voice to the voiceless, but at the same time, enjoying writing for the gratification of penning my thoughts and capturing that memorable moment in time.

I write what I feel and see, and at rare moments, what I imagine. I do live in your world, but I hope you like my mind. I think so i am

Please watch out for Your World, My Mind Part 2.

About The Author

Sam The Word, the author, hails from the East Midlands, often humorously referred to as "Middle Earth," where Leicester shines as a geographical gem of England.

His journey as a writer commenced 27 years ago, albeit temporarily interrupted when a digital organizer mishap wiped away his cherished poem about Black Jesus.

Life took an unexpected turn in the year 2000 when he found himself remanded at Doncaster's Premiere Category A prison.

During this time, two beloved poems were lost due to a mandatory transfer to the Beruit Wing.

Despite these challenges, he was handed a life sentence, but it wasn't the end of his writing journey.

Sam The Word rekindled his passion for writing, initially oblivious to the art of poetry and the strict rules of grammar and punctuation governing novels.

He proudly stood as an anti-establishment figure, showing minimal regard for conformity.

Fearing he might compromise the raw truth of his expression, he persevered.

Although he now possesses a Tefl English teaching certificate, he still primarily writes as his thoughts and emotions flow, though he has come to appreciate the structured nature of the English language through tutorials.

Readers can expect to encounter his abstract writing style, characterized by realism and occasional humor.

Sam The Word's work holds socio-political and historical significance, offering a refreshing departure from the often stuffy, pretentious prose and poetry that have irked him.

Writing became his sanctuary and means of escape.

Within his artistic expression, Sam The Word presents a unique perspective on the concept of a "flat Earth," offering a narrative that diverges from the mundane, politically correct clichés frequently regurgitated by the media and the general public.

In "Your World My Mind," he pulls no punches, giving voice to thoughts that many hold but fear to articulate, particularly concerning the contentious issue of race. The title, "Your World My Mind," aptly encapsulates this thought-provoking journey.

www.ingramcontent.com/pod-product-compliance
Lightning Source LLC
Chambersburg PA
CBRC091722070526
44585CB00007B/146